THE GOLF SETUP, DISTILLED

Illustrated Guide to a Perfect Setup

PETE STYLES

Published by
Golf Distillery - Extracting the Essence of Golf

Ebook ISBN: 978-1-7774183-5-9
Paperback ISBN: 978-1-7774183-3-5
Hardcover ISBN: 978-1-7774183-4-2

Golf Distillery

TABLE OF CONTENTS

INTRODUCTION

to the "Golf, Distilled" Series

I have a passionate belief that anyone can play consistently great golf. That belief comes from delivering thousands of lessons to players from every walk of life and at every level.

What I've found is that when you commit just a short amount of time to really ingraining the proven fundamentals of golf, it transforms your game.

Fundamentals might not be new. They might not seem exciting either – especially when you read about "magic moves" and "undiscovered swing secrets" in glossy magazines and elsewhere on the internet.

But mastering the fundamentals is exciting. Very exciting. Why? Because it delivers.

It gives you everything you want from the game – solid, crisp ball striking, booming drives that split the fairway in two, penetrating irons, masterful touch and feel and of course... consistency – in every area of your game.

I'm sure you already know that golfers can spend years chasing one gimmick after another without seeing any long-term improvement in their game. The irony is that if they just spent a fraction of that time mastering the key fundamentals of golf, they'd have a great swing... a swing for life.

That's the aim of this series of illustrated guides: to inspire you to become the great golfer you can be... and to give you step-by-step lessons to help achieve it!

Pete Styles, PGA Class A Professional
Over 75 000 lessons delivered
Manchester, England, UK

THE GOLF SETUP, DISTILLED

ILLUSTRATED GUIDE TO A PERFECT GOLF SETUP

This book covers everything you need for a great golf setup position. There are a number of key elements in the golf setup:

- Proper alignment
- The correct stance and ball position
- Good posture
- A correct grip

The next sections look at each of these in more detail. But before you jump ahead, it's worth really appreciating why a proper setup position is so critical to your golf game.

NEVER UNDERESTIMATE THE IMPORTANCE OF YOUR SETUP

To understand why your setup is so important, it's useful to understand a bit about open and closed skills in sport.

An **open skill** involves variables that are usually beyond your control. Think of a tackle in soccer – you have to react to the movements of other players and a moving ball.

A **closed skill** on the other hand is controlled purely by you. Think of a free throw in basketball – there are no moving players to contend with, the ball is stationary and there are no real time constraints.

Any sport that is made up of closed skills usually demands you to be very accurate and very consistent (think of darts, pool, shooting etc). The golf swing is a closed skill – and one with a very small margin of error. Because of this we have to take every precaution to maximize our accuracy and consistency. The starting point for this consistency is our setup.

By repeating the same setup every time for every shot, we allow our golf swing to develop as quickly and as consistently as possible. Any variation and faults in our golf setup routine will have a detrimental effect on the outcome of each shot.

I would encourage all golfers of any standard to continually focus on a good quality setup. You should pay particular attention to accurate alignment (see the first section below) as it's an area I feel many golfers overlook and lack discipline in establishing it as part of their setup routine.

ALIGNMENT

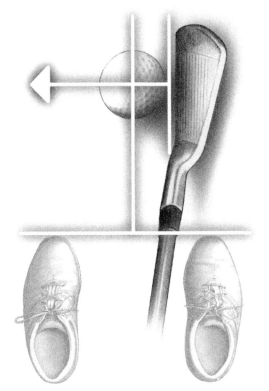

HOW TO LINE UP A GOLF SHOT

In the first part of this setup guide, we'll look at proper golf alignment.

Even though most amateur golfers understand the importance of lining themselves up correctly on the golf course (and have a fair idea what it consists of), I still see alignment issues in the majority of players I meet. There are 2 reasons for this:

1. They have altered their stance and address position to try and compensate for a fault in their golf swing (such as a slice).
2. They simply fail to check their alignment on a very regular basis and bad habits silently creep in.

In this section, we'll recap what proper alignment consists of. I'd also like to offer you some tips and advice for maintaining a great setup position throughout your golfing career.

A consistent golf swing and a consistent golf game can only be built on proper alignment. Don't try and correct faults in your game before addressing this issue.

Follow the tips below to remind yourself how to line up to the ball and target correctly:

- To check your alignment, pick a target in the distance and set up to the ball as normal. Place a club along the line of your toes, step back and see where the club points:

- If the club points directly at the target, or to the right of the target, your stance is what we call **closed**.

- If the club points way left of the target, your stance is what we call **open**.

- The club should point **parallel left** of the target (imagine the line along your feet and the line from the ball to the target are like 2 train tracks). This is a **square** stance.

- Remember your knees, hips and shoulders should be in line or parallel to your feet. If you can, have a friend hold a golf club across your hips and then your shoulders while you are in the setup position. Step away and check where this club is pointing.

- Don't forget the angle of the clubface as you address the golf ball. This should be square (at right angles) to the ball-to-target line.

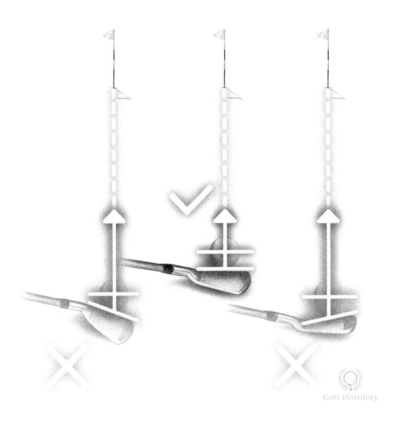

MAKE GREAT GOLF ALIGNMENT FEEL LIKE SECOND NATURE

Proper alignment on the golf course isn't a technically difficult subject – it's common sense. But because it's so basic, I think that's why so many club golfers forget to check it on a regular basis.

Tour Pros check their own alignment every time they practice. It's not too basic for them so it shouldn't be for any other standard of golfer (who are more likely to fall into bad habits in the first place). Here are a few tips for ingraining great alignment into your game:

1. Each time you visit the range, check the position of your feet, knees, hips and shoulders. Place a couple of clubs or alignment sticks along the ground as a visual reference.
2. If possible, ask someone to stand behind you as you hit balls and ask them to check your hips and shoulders (as these are more difficult to check yourself).
3. Standing behind the ball looking at your target, pick a mark a few feet in front of the golf ball that is directly on your ball-to-target line (it could be a leaf or a patch of dark grass for example). Set up as normal and imagine a line running from your ball to this mark. Adjust your

feet, hips and shoulders so they are parallel to this line.

4. Practice with a spare club in the house or office 3-5 times a day for 7-10 days. Run through the routine of standing behind your ball, picking a mark and lining up parallel to that mark. This can then become part of your pre-shot routine on the golf course to ensure you line up to every shot correctly.

STANCE

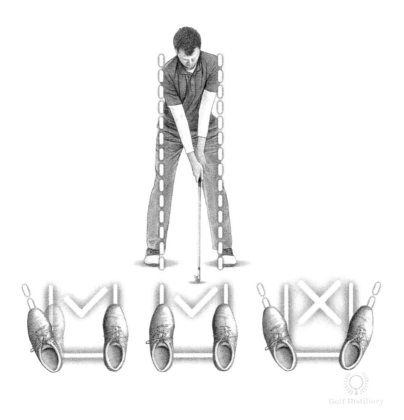

HOW TO POSITION YOUR FEET FOR EVERY CLUB

Now that you've checked your alignment and have yourself pointing in the right direction, the next step is to build a proper golf stance.

A golf stance is made up of several elements – the right width of stance, the right amount of knee flex, the angle of the feet and overall posture. We'll look at posture in part 6 of this guide.

A stance that is too narrow will prevent you from generating a lot of power in your golf swing. It will also make it difficult to keep your balance – which can severely compromise your ball striking.

But I see some golfers go too far the other way.

If your stance is too wide, you'll find it difficult to shift your body weight during the swing (essential for power, timing and ball striking) and if you do, it will be more of a sway (something we want to avoid).

- To ensure the correct width of your stance, measure the width of your shoulders using a club. Then make sure the **insides** of your feet are at least this wide apart for all full shots.

- Widen your stance (insides of feet are 2-3 inches wider than shoulder width) for longer clubs such as fairway woods and the driver.

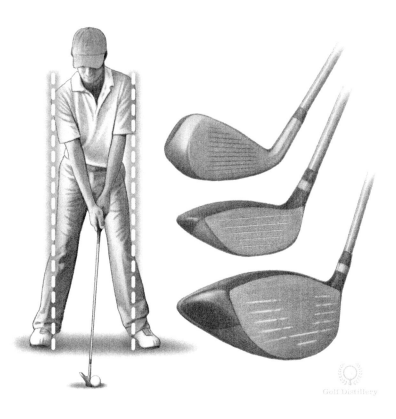

- Reduce your stance width by an inch or two for short irons and wedges. For less than full shots, i.e. pitching and chipping, we don't need a wide stance.

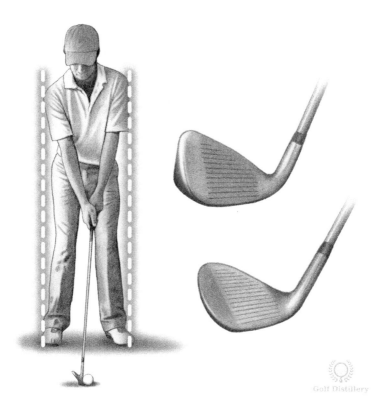

- Avoid pointing your toes out at too much of an angle. Your rear foot should be at right angles to the target line. Your front foot can be angled outwards but only slightly.

- Knees should be lightly flexed but not bent.

- Your body weight should be spread 50/50 between your toes and heels as well as 50/50 between your left and right foot for most shots.

DISTANCE TO THE BALL

HOW FAR/CLOSE SHOULD YOU BE FROM THE BALL

So far in this golf setup guide, we've looked at your alignment and your stance. The next stage is to look at the distance you set up to the golf ball.

Because each club in the bag is a different length, our distance to the golf ball is going to change accordingly.

In time, you'll develop a natural feel for the correct distance with each club, but I'd like to give you a specific method to test you're in a good position.

- Address the golf ball and lock your knees – so there is no flex in your knees at all. You should feel your weight shift towards your heels.

- Now, just flex your knees slightly until you feel your weight shift from your heels towards the balls of your feet. When you feel your weight is balanced over the centre of your feet, that's enough knee flex.

- Take the chosen club and lower it onto your front thigh. The club should touch about **1 inch above your kneecap**. If this doesn't happen, alter your distance to the golf ball as necessary.

- Remember not to flex or straighten your leg to get the club resting an inch above the kneecap – you need to move your feet further or closer to the ball.

DISTANCE TO THE BALL

BALL POSITION

WHERE TO POSITION THE BALL IN YOUR STANCE

In part 4 of this golf setup guide, we'll look at the correct golf ball position for each club.

We've just covered the correct distance to the golf ball and a quick test that you can use to make sure you're not setting up too close or too far away.

This section looks at the ideal golf ball position **between your feet**– whether the ball should sit centrally between your feet or closer to your left or right foot.

The position of the golf ball actually changes depending on the club you're using. The reason for this is that we want to slightly change the impact position and the launch conditions so that we get the best ball flight for the club in hand.

- Take your correct width of stance and place a club directly in the centre, at right angles to the ball-to-target line. This central position is the ideal position for the shortest clubs in your bag – lob wedge, sand wedge, gap wedge, pitching wedge etc. It helps us to hit down on the ball creating more backspin.

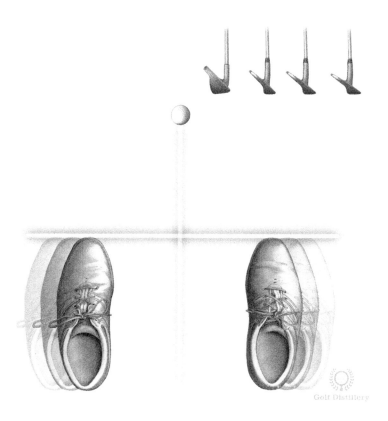

- For each longer club, the ball position should move roughly **half an inch** towards your front foot (left foot for right-handed golfers). So a 7-iron for example, would be played a couple of inches off centre, towards your front foot.

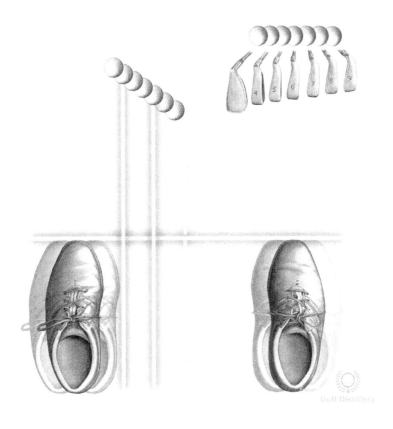

BALL POSITION

- The longest club in the bag, the driver, should be played just inside the front foot or opposite the left big toe (again for the right-handed golfer). This allows us to sweep the ball away rather than hitting down on it.

- The golf ball position should also move closer and further away from the body with each club – because each club is a different length. For a quick and easy method of positioning the golf ball the right distance from you, refer to part 3 of this guide (i.e., Correct Distance to the Golf Ball).

POSITION OF THE HANDS

WHERE TO POSITION YOUR HANDS

The position of the hands at setup, in relation to the golf ball, can help to determine the quality of your ball striking.

In the previous instalments of this golf setup guide, we've looked at the correct ball position for each club (part 4), and the ideal distance you should be standing away from the golf ball (part 3).

There's one more checkpoint that I see a lot of golfers overlook (even lower handicap players) that you should incorporate into your setup position. It has to do with the position of your hands at address in relation to the golf ball. It's a very simple tip but it can make a noticeable difference to your golf game.

- To ensure that your setup mimics your impact position, **point the butt end of the club at your front or left hip**.

- Having the club held too far back may promote scooping. It can also cause you to hit the ball fat or thin.

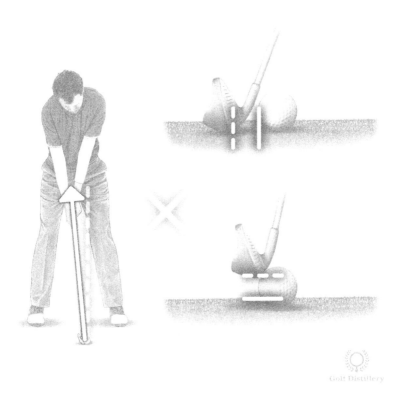

POSITION OF THE HANDS

- Likewise, having the club held too far forward would also result in inconsistent strikes and a ball flight that is too low.

POSTURE

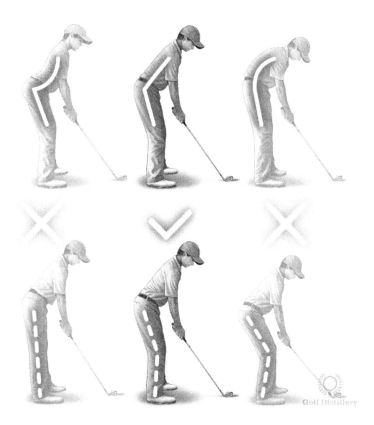

HOW TO POSITION YOURSELF ON TOP OF THE BALL

Great golf posture is crucial for consistent, accurate and powerful ball striking.

You don't have to be an athlete to achieve great posture over the ball and the tips on this section will work for golfers of all shapes and sizes.

The golf swing is essentially a turning motion around a central column – that central column being your spine. The better the position and the angle of your spine at address, the better it will be throughout the swing, especially at impact.

Now, different people will have different natural postures. Your posture might not be great while you're sitting, standing or driving for example, but with a little bit of practice you can create a very efficient stance over the golf ball.

Here's how to correct a poor posture position (that is either slumped or too upright):

- Hold the club in front of your belly button with your arms and legs straight. Stand up tall with your shoulders pulled back and stick your chest out.

- Tilt forwards making sure you tilt at the **hips only**. Your lower back should remain flat rather than rounded. Feel like you are pushing your behind backwards.

- As the club lowers to touch the ground behind the ball, **flex your knees slightly**. Avoid making the mistake of many amateur golfers by over-bending your knees.

GRIP

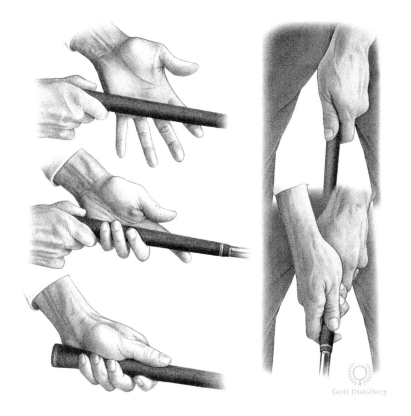

HOW TO GRIP THE GOLF CLUB

The importance of a proper golf grip is one of the most written about topics in golf instruction. Yet most golfers that come to see me for the first time, grip a golf club in a way that is costing them power, accuracy and consistency.

Remember, your grip is your only link to the golf club.

That golf ball you're about to hit – it doesn't react to what your swing looks like or how you're standing or how long you've been playing golf.

All it reacts to is:

1. *how fast* the club is travelling,
2. *what direction* the club is travelling in and
3. the *position of the clubface* at impact.

All of those are controlled by how you grip the golf club.

Yes, changing your golf grip is uncomfortable at first and you might feel like you've taken a step backwards in the immediate term. But it's well worth the small amount of effort it takes to make a proper golf grip feel second nature. You'll play much more consistent, solid golf for many years to come as a result.

A correct golf grip will help you to achieve more distance, greater feel, better ball striking and more consistency with every club in your bag. Follow these steps for a great grip (reverse the instructions if you are left-handed):

LEFT HAND

- Place the club in the fingers of the left hand. The grip of the club should run from the **middle of the index finger to the base of the little finger**.

- Grip the club **half an inch from the end**. Compared to gripping it right at the end, this will improve your control of the club and ball striking ability, without any loss of power.

- As you look down at your left hand, there should be **2½ knuckles** visible. This is classed as **neutral** position. The 'V' made by your left thumb and forefinger should **point to your right shoulder**.

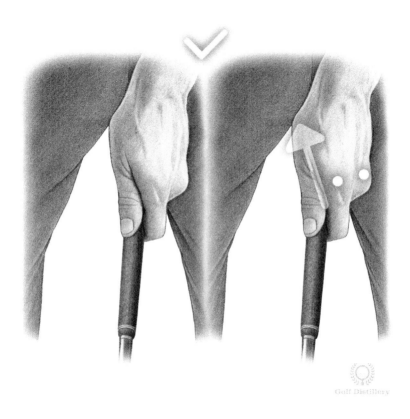

- If you can see **more than 2½ knuckles**, your left hand is said to be in **too strong** a position.

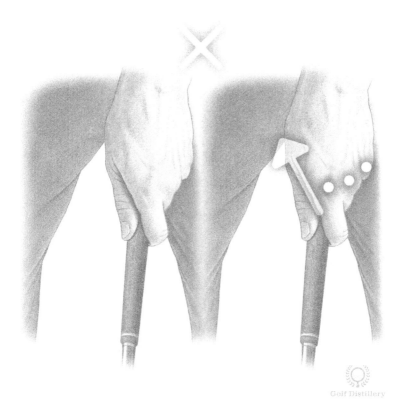

- If you can see **less than 2½ knuckles**, your left hand is in **too weak** a position.

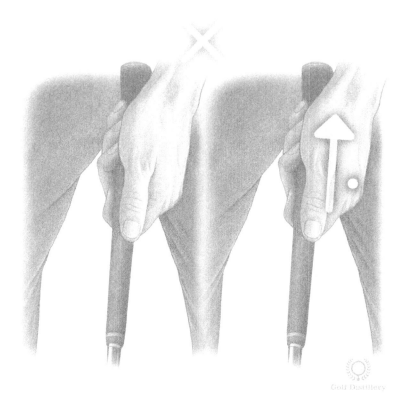

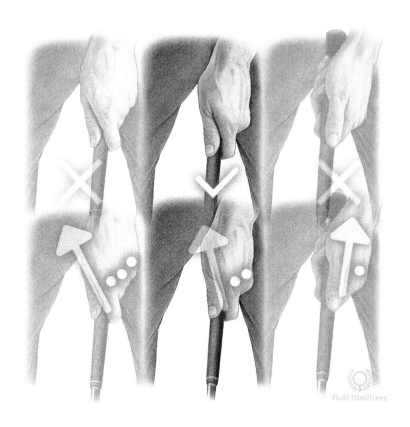

RIGHT HAND

- Place the fleshy pad of your right thumb **directly on top of your left thumb**.

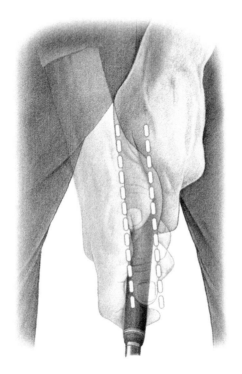

- The 'V' made between your right thumb and forefinger should **point to your chin.**

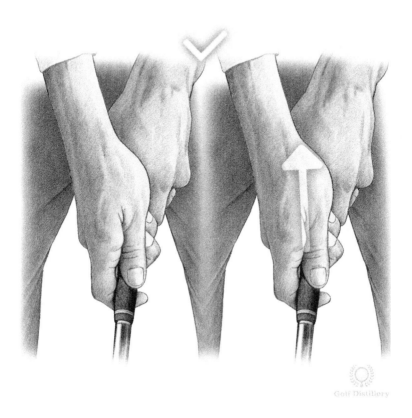

- If the 'V' points **over your right shoulder**, your right hand is in **too strong** a position.

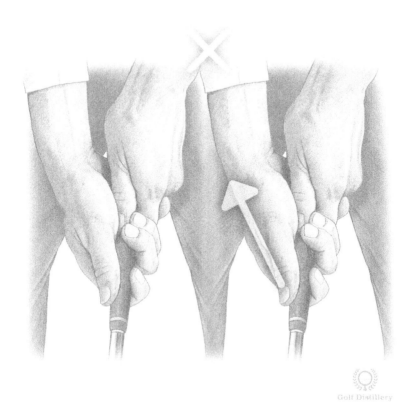

- If the 'V' points **over your left shoulder**, your right hand is in **too weak** a position.

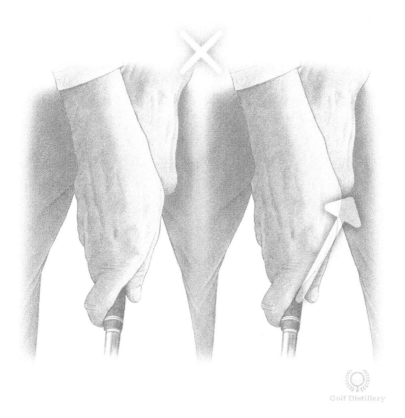

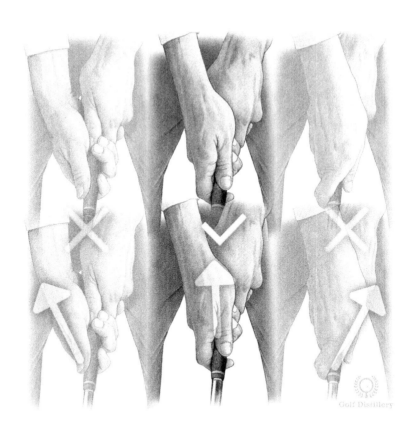

THE 3 TYPES OF GOLF GRIPS

- The fingers of the right hand can grip the club and link with the left hand in 3 different ways – referred to as the **overlapping** (or 'Vardon' grip), the **interlinking** grip, and the **baseball** grip.

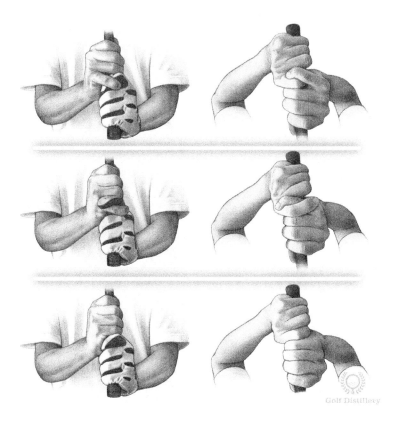

- It's a common misconception amongst amateur golfers that the interlinking grip is predominantly used by ladies and juniors. Both Jack Nicklaus and Tiger Woods have used the interlinking grip.

- I recommend you use either the interlinking or overlapping grip – whichever you find more comfortable.

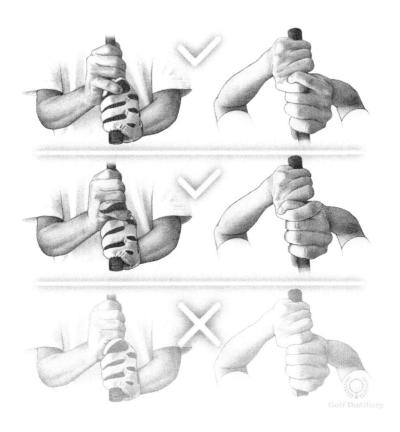

GRIP PRESSURE – HOW HARD SHOULD YOU GRIP THE GOLF CLUB?

- You'll often hear that gripping the club tightly causes tension in the body, which in turn hinders your ability to make a good swing. However, gripping the club with a lot of pressure at the point of impact will help you to better control the strike.

- On a scale of 1 to 10, imagine that a level 10 equates to gripping the club as tightly as possible. A level 1 equates to holding the club so loosely it only just stays in your hands.

- **At address**, hold the club with a grip pressure of **4 out of 10**.

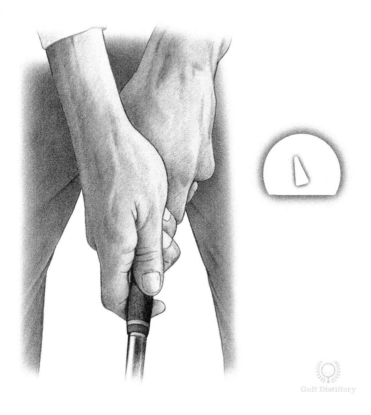

- **At impact**, your grip pressure should increase to a **9 or even a 10 out of 10**. You might want to consciously grasp the club more tightly at impact to see how that effects your ball striking.

BONUS - TOP 10 TIPS FOR BEGINNERS

#1: TAKE DEAD AIM

Not just for your feet but also knees, hips, shoulders and clubface. Most right-handed golfers aim right but this doesn't always mean the ball will go right as often their swing will compensate for poor alignment. Check your alignment every practice session for the rest of your life!

#2: CREATE A SOLID STANCE

Create a stance which is wide, solid, stable and balanced.
Build your golf swing from the ground up.

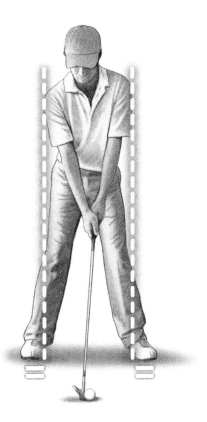

#3: DEVELOP PERFECT POSTURE

Focus on great posture by tilting at your hips and not at your waist.

#4: MAKE FRIENDS WITH YOUR GRIP

Practice holding the club in the correct position even when you are not playing golf. Take a club into the house and every time you walk past it hold it for 30 seconds and soon your hands will be married to the club correctly.

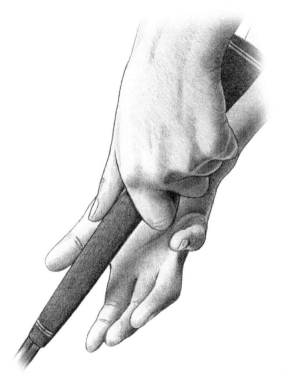

#5: START YOUR DOWNSWING WITH YOUR HIPS

Nearly every downswing fault is due to starting it with the upper body rather than 'bumping the hips'. Imagine skimming a stone or throwing a baseball and how the lower body starts the movement with the upper body following.

#6: MAKE RANGE SESSIONS COUNT

Learn your trade on the driving range before you head for the course. Each range session should include 50 balls and should last at least 30 minutes with two practice swings for every ball. Practice with purpose.

#7: USE PLENTY OF LOFT

Practicing with a short, lofted club encourages better posture and cleaner ball striking. Everybody gains confidence in seeing a nice high ball flight. Too little loft encourages new golfers to use a destructive scooping action to get the ball upwards.

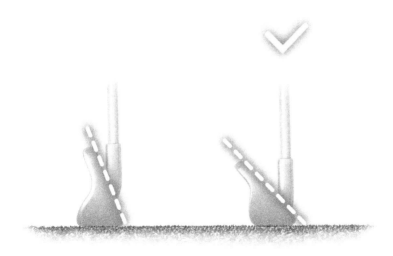

#8: LEAVE THE DRIVER IN THE BAG

Start your practice sessions with your pitching wedge and move through your bag of clubs mastering each one as you go. Avoid using a longer and more difficult club until you are consistently and confidently hitting the shorter ones. Many golfers would be better to avoid the driver for at least the first 18 months of playing!

#9: TRY A PAR-3 COURSE

Par-3 courses are great to develop your understanding of the game and your course management skills. You'll spend less time looking for golf balls and you'll begin to hone those all-important short-game skills.

#10: REVIEW MY FUNDAMENTALS ONCE A MONTH

As your interest in golf grows, you'll begin to read golf magazines, watch golf infomercials and be tempted by "revolutionary golf swing programs" on the Internet.

If you're not careful, you can fall into the trap of chasing that many different techniques and opinions that you end up with a disjointed golf swing and a head full of conflicting thoughts.

The address position fundamentals you have learned in this *The Golf Setup, Distilled* are proven and time-served. Stick to them. For the swing fundamentals, you'll find them in *The Golf Swing, Distilled*.

YOUTUBE CHANNEL LINK

For more golf tips,
visit our YouTube channel:

www.golfdistillery.com

ALSO BY GOLF DISTILLERY

Continue on your quest to better golf with these:

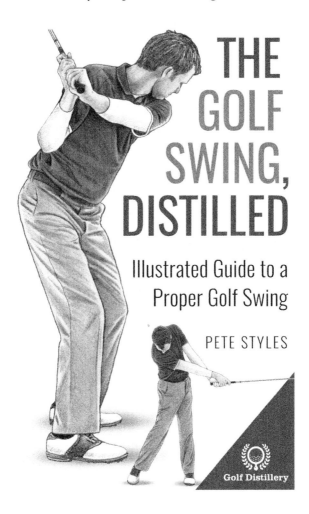

THE GOLF SWING, DISTILLED

Illustrated Guide to a Proper Golf Swing

PETE STYLES

Golf Distillery

6 WEEKS TO GOLF FITNESS

How to Get Healthy and Fit, and Hit the Ball Further Than Ever

PHIL DAVIES

Golf Distillery

GOLF

THROUGH THE EYES
OF A CHILD

Written by
Dominique DeSerres

Illustrated by
Aga Kubish

Golf Distillery

PERSONAL NOTES

PERSONAL NOTES

PERSONAL NOTES

Printed in Great Britain
by Amazon

44023506R00056